Read-About® Geography

Great Lakes

By Kimberly Valzania

Consultant
Nanci R. Vargus, Ed.D.
Assistant Professor of Literacy
University of Indianapolis
Indianapolis, Indiana

Children's Press®
A Division of Scholastic Inc.
New York   Toronto   London   Auckland   Sydney
Mexico City   New Delhi   Hong Kong
Danbury, Connecticut

Designer: Herman Adler Design
Photo Researcher: Caroline Anderson
The photo on the cover shows a satellite image of the Great Lakes.

Library of Congress Cataloging-in-Publication Data

Valzania, Kim.
  Great Lakes / by Kimberly Valzania.
      p. cm. – (Rookie read-about geography)
  Includes index.
  Summary: A brief introduction to the Great Lakes, describing how they were
formed, plants and animals found there, how people use the Great Lakes, and
efforts to keep them clean.
    ISBN 0-516-22758-0 (lib. bdg.)   0-516-24648-8 (pbk.)
    1. Great Lakes–Juvenile literature. 2. Great Lakes Region–Juvenile
literature. 3. Great Lakes Region—Geography—Juvenile literature. [1.
Great Lakes. 2. Great Lakes Region.] I. Title. II. Series.
  F551.V35 2004
  977—dc22
                                    2003016933

CHILDREN'S PRESS, and ROOKIE READ-ABOUT®,
and associated logos are trademarks and or registered trademarks
of Scholastic Library Publishing. SCHOLASTIC and associated logos
are trademarks and or registered trademarks of Scholastic Inc.
1 2 3 4 5 6 7 8 9 10 R 13 12 11 10 09 08 07 06 05 04

Inch by inch, a glacier (GLAY-shur) moves.

A glacier is a river of ice. It moves slowly. As it moves, it carves large holes under the ice.

Long ago, glaciers
moved across parts
of North America.

Then, temperatures
became warmer. The
glaciers began to shrink.

They left large holes
in the land. The holes
filled with water.

These holes became the
five Great Lakes. You will
find them between the
United States and Canada.

They are so big, you can
see them from space!

Lake Michigan

10

Oceans are filled with salty water. The Great Lakes are filled with fresh water.

Almost all of the fresh water in the United States is in the Great Lakes.

Lake Superior (suh-PEER-ee-uhr) is the largest of the five Great Lakes.

It is also the coldest and the deepest.

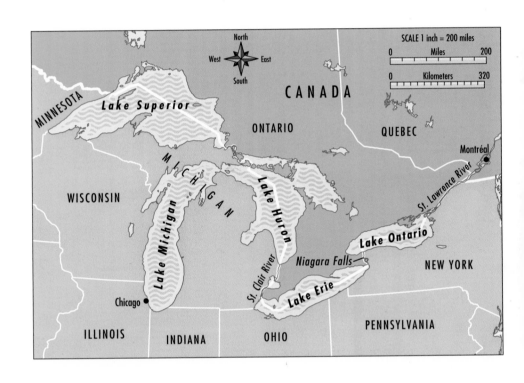

North
West · East
South

SCALE 1 inch = 200 miles
0   Miles   200
0   Kilometers   320

CANADA

MINNESOTA

Lake Superior

ONTARIO

QUEBEC

Montréal

WISCONSIN

M I C H I G A N

Lake Michigan

Lake Huron

St. Lawrence River

Lake Ontario

St. Clair River

Niagara Falls

NEW YORK

Chicago •

Lake Erie

ILLINOIS

INDIANA

OHIO

PENNSYLVANIA

13

"Mighty Mac" bridge

Lake Michigan (MISH-uh-guhn) is the next largest lake. All of Lake Michigan is inside the United States.

The "Mighty Mac" bridge joins Lake Michigan and Lake Huron (HYUR-uhn).

Lake Huron has many islands. One of them is Mackinac Island.

The largest island is called Manitoulin (man-uh-TOO-lin). It is the largest island of any lake in the world.

Mackinac Island

The St. Clair River flows from Lake Huron to Lake Erie (EER-ee). The river makes a waterway between the lakes.

The walleye lives in Lake Erie.

Walleye

In 1825, the Erie Canal (kuh–NAL) opened. The canal let ocean ships sail to all of the lakes.

The ships carried settlers, crops, and logs.

Lake Ontario (AHN-tare-ee-oh) is the smallest lake. It sits below the Niagara Falls.

Some water from the Niagara River is carried away in tunnels. Then, it is used to make electricity.

The Saint Lawrence River starts in Lake Ontario. This river is an important waterway.

Today, ships use it to carry people and goods. They stop at busy cities like Chicago and Montréal.

Many people live near the Great Lakes. They need the lakes for drinking water and electric power.

They use the lakes to ship loads of steel, copper, and food.

Many people play on the lakes, too.

You can cross a bridge, or catch a fish. You can play on the beach, or ride on a boat.

What would you do if you went to the Great Lakes?

Words You Know

bridge

canal

glacier

islands

waterfall

waterway

Index

About the Author

Kimberly Valzania writes educational materials for students preparing to take standardized tests in English, social studies, math, and science. She enjoys writing nonfiction for younger students and has contributed other books in the Rookie Read-About® Geography series. She lives and works in Connecticut.

Photo Credits

Photographs © 2004: Corbis Images: 25, 31 bottom right (William A. Bake), 14, 30 top (W. Cody), 17, 31 top right (Layne Kennedy); Dembinsky Photo Assoc.: 26 (Sharon Cummings), 10 (Barbara Gerlach), 29 (Stephen Graham), 17 (Gary Meszaros), 9 (NASA); North Wind Picture Archives: 21, 30 bottom; Photo Researchers, NY: 5 (Carlyn Iverson), cover (WorldSat International/SS); Superstock, Inc./Steve Vidler: 22, 31 bottom left; The Image Works: 6 (Sonda Dawes), 3, 31 top left (Topham).

Map by Bob Italiano